GW00514806

IN
MEMORY
OF

Curious Cats

Yoda — April 1986 To
        NOVEMBER 2002.

Charlie — 19th April 1987 To
          13th February 2003.

George — 19th April 1987 To
         13th May 2003.

Other books
by Bob Walker and Frances Mooney

The Cats' House

Cats into Everything

Crazy Cats

Comical Cats

Curious Cats

Bob Walker and Frances Mooney

**Andrews McMeel
Publishing**

Kansas City

Curious Cats

For information, write Andrews McMeel Publishing,
an Andrews McMeel Universal company,
4520 Main Street, Kansas City, Missouri 64111.

Book design by Holly Camerlinck

ISBN: 0-7407-1460-0

Library of Congress Card Number:
00-108403

www.catshouse.com

Cats are curious creatures

that can be many things . . .

sweet

whiskery

thoughtful

dreamy

incandescent

fireballs

innocent

troublemakers

slurped

self-cleaning

sniffers

nibblers

copycats

fearless

hunters

florists

sun worshippers

studious

secretive

eavesdroppers

forgiving

helpful

comforters

well-fed

chug-a-luggers

fishers

slurpers

moochers

distant

dreamers

lazybones

nosy

adorable

angelic

weightless

buddies

heaters

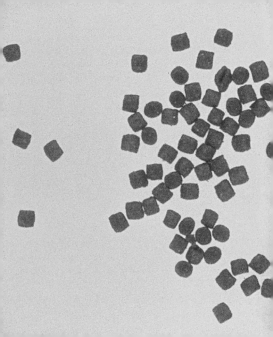